Aebleskiver and More

A Sampling of Danish Recipes

Edited by Lisa Steen Riggs
Director, Danish Windmill, Elk Horn, Iowa

Cover photographs by Joan Liffring-Zug Bourret
Drawings by Diane Heusinkveld

Senior editors: Dorothy Crum and Maureen Patterson
Associate editors: Miriam Canter, Melinda Bradnan, and Kelly Nelson

Penfield
BOOKS

This collection of Danish recipes, inspired by the puffy round æbleskiver, is an expression of the creative spirit of the Danish cook. Ordinary mealtimes become succulent feasts. Penfield Books thanks Lisa Steen Riggs, director, and her staff at the Danish Windmill historic site, Elk Horn, Iowa; contributors noted with their individual recipes; and friends, including Oluf Davidsen.

The Æbleskiver Pan

Not usually found in the "ordinary" kitchen, the 6-1/2-inch, cast-iron æbleskiver pan has seven round holes and fits over a stove burner. The pan can be found in most Scandinavian specialty or other gourmet food shops. It is a popular item at the Danish Windmill Gift Shop, P.O. Box 245, Elk Horn, Iowa. E-mail address: info@danishwindmill.com. Website: www.danishwindmill.com

ISBN-13: 978-193204318-1
ISBN-10: 193204318-7
©Copyright 2003 Penfield Books
www.penfieldbooks.com

Contents

The Danish Windmill

In 1975 a group of enterprising residents of the Elk Horn, Iowa, area purchased the 60-foot, eight-sided windmill, which had been in Norre Snede, Jutland, Denmark, for 127 years. The mill was dismantled by Danish carpenters, shipped to Elk Horn, and rebuilt in 1976 by community volunteers to honor the area's Danish heritage. Today visitors can tour the mill compound, climb to the top of the working mill, see the grinding stones, and watch the wings go around on a windy day.

The mill grinds locally grown wheat, rye, and corn, which is sold to visitors in the adjoining gift shop, proclaimed as the largest Danish gift shop in the United States. The Danish villages of Elk Horn and Kimballton make up the largest rural Danish settlement. The Windmill is "a piece of Denmark close to home."

The Danish Immigrant Museum

Situated on a 20-acre site in Elk Horn, Iowa, the beautiful, modern 16,000-square-foot building housing the museum is reminiscent of Danish half-timbered architecture. The museum was founded in 1983 and dedicated in 1994. The museum's mission is to tell the story of the Danish-American experience and to preserve the rich culture, traditions, and heritage that Danish immigrants have brought to America over the past century and a half. Share the story and experience of early Danish immigrants, beginning with their decision to leave Denmark to the establishment of new homes, schools, churches, and settlements in America as you tour the self-guiding, permanent exhibition *Across Oceans, Across Time.* For visitor information write: The Danish Immigrant Museum, 2212 Washington Street, Box 470, Elk Horn, IA 51531; call toll free 1-877-764-7008; or e-mail info@danishmuseum.org.

Other Sites of Interest

Grand View College in Des Moines, Iowa, and Dana College at Blair, Nebraska, both have strong Danish roots.

Greenville, Michigan, has an annual Danish festival.

Mount Rushmore in South Dakota is the work of Danish-American Gutzon Borglum.

Racine, Wisconsin, is noted for great bakeries, especially The O & H Bakery. Its blueberry and almond pecan kringles are our favorites.

Solvang, California, is north of Santa Barbara in the Santa Ynez mountains. Tourists from all over the world enjoy this storybook town with its windmills, folk art scenes of characters from Hans Christian Andersen's fairy tales, great shopping, and wonderful restaurants. Rasmussen's Solvang specializes in Danish gifts and books. The Book Nook is a wonderful place to treat the mind.

Tyler, Minnesota, is the home of an old stone hall, once used as a schoolhouse. Currently, it is used as a Danish heritage education center.

Rasmussen's Solvang
Solvang, California

 Æbleskiver

Æbleskiver

This Danish delicacy is served in many Danish-American homes. A special pan is needed; even though new pans are available, many cooks favor the old cast-iron pans, which are handed down from generation to generation. Many communities have æbleskiver festivals as fund-raisers. In Denmark, æbleskiver are served as a dessert with sugar or marmalade. On the island of Ærø, a small sliver of prune is put in the middle as they are cooked. Everyone has a favorite recipe so we have included the best of the best.

You will need a little practice in turning these doughnut-like treats. A fork works, but some practiced "turners" use a knitting needle, preferably wooden, or a similar device such as an ice pick. Even a toothpick will do. Be creative.

Great Grandma's Danish Æbleskiver

2 cups flour
1 teaspoon salt
1 teaspoon baking soda

2 cups buttermilk
3 eggs, separated
Powdered sugar for sprinkling

Sift together flour, salt, and baking soda. Add buttermilk and egg yolks. Beat egg whites until light and fluffy, forming soft peaks. Gently fold egg whites into batter. Heat æbleskiver pan on medium heat. Grease each cup with a little butter, oil, or vegetable spray and fill 2/3 full. Cook for approximately 1 to 1-1/2 minutes per side until golden brown; flip using a toothpick. When both sides are done, serve with a sprinkle of powdered sugar. Best when served warm.

Optional: Fill each cup only 1/3 full with batter; place a small amount of fruit in each cup and cover with additional batter.

Lemon-flavored Æbleskiver

6 eggs
2-1/2 cups buttermilk
1-1/2 teaspoons lemon extract
3 cups flour

3/4 teaspoon baking soda
2 tablespoons baking powder
1-1/2 teaspoons salt
Oil for baking

Beat eggs and buttermilk together until cream-colored. Add remaining ingredients separately and mix after each addition. Heat pan on high heat. Pour about 1 teaspoon of oil into each cup. A basting brush works well to coat each cup. Re-oil pan for each batch. Fill cups nearly to the brim with batter. When batter begins to bubble around the edges and sides begin to cook, use a skewer to turn. Continually turn the æbleskiver in all directions, so that they cook evenly. Remove when they are a dark, golden brown. Serve with powdered or granulated sugar.

Quick Æbleskiver

4 cups Bisquick baking mix
3 cups milk

4 eggs, slightly beaten
Oil for baking

Combine all ingredients, being careful not to stir too much. Heat æbleskiver pan until hot. Pour 1 tablespoon of oil into each cup. Fill each cup with batter. As batter cooks, turn with a fine knitting needle or ice pick, forming a round ball. Turn slowly and bake thoroughly until dark, golden brown.

Bedstemor's Æbleskiver

4 eggs, separated
2 tablespoons butter
1 teaspoon salt
1/4 cup sugar

2 cups flour
2 cups buttermilk
2 teaspoons baking soda
Nutmeg or lemon extract (optional)

Beat egg yolks, butter, salt, and sugar together. Add flour, buttermilk, baking soda, and nutmeg or lemon extract as desired. Beat until batter is smooth. Beat egg whites until stiff, then fold into batter. In a well-greased æbleskiver pan, fill holes 3/4 full. When half done, turn with a fork or sharp knitting needle and cook until lightly browned.

Note: Serve with jelly and a sprinkle of powdered sugar, or top with a teaspoon of applesauce during last half of cooking.

Buttermilk Æbleskiver

3 eggs, separated
2 cups buttermilk
1-1/2 cups flour
2 teaspoons baking powder

1 tablespoon sugar
1/2 teaspoon salt
2 tablespoons melted butter
Oil or shortening for baking

Beat egg whites until stiff; set aside. Beat egg yolks and buttermilk together. Sift dry ingredients together and add to liquid mixture; add the melted butter and mix together until smooth. Fold in the beaten egg whites. Fill pan cups about 1/4 full of oil or shortening; heat and fill with batter. When batter begins to bubble around edges, turn with fork and continue turning until evenly brown. **To test:** Fork inserted in center will come out clean.

Æbleskiver with Cardamom

3 eggs, separated
2 cups milk
1-1/2 cups flour
2 teaspoons baking powder
1 tablespoon sugar

1/2 teaspoon salt
1/8 to 1/4 teaspoon cardamom
2 tablespoons melted butter
Oil or shortening for baking

Beat egg whites until stiff; set aside. Beat egg yolks. Add milk. Sift dry ingredients together and add to liquid mixture. Add the melted butter and fold in beaten egg whites. Pour a generous amount of oil into holes of æbleskiver pan and heat; fill with batter and bake until edges are bubbly. Turn and continue turning until evenly browned and fork inserted in center comes out clean.

Yeast Æbleskiver

2 cups milk
1 tablespoon butter
2 packages dry yeast
1/2 cup lukewarm water
4 eggs, separated
2 tablespoons sugar

1/2 teaspoon salt
1 teaspoon cinnamon
1/4 teaspoon cardamom
2-1/2 cups flour
Oil or shortening for baking

Scald milk, add butter, and let cool. Dissolve yeast in the 1/2 cup of warm water. Beat egg yolks; add the milk mixture, sugar, salt, spices, yeast, and flour. Set aside to let rise for 30 minutes. When ready to bake, beat egg whites until stiff and fold very gently into batter. Pour generous amount of oil into holes of æbleskiver pan; heat. Fill with batter and bake until edges are bubbly. Turn and continue turning until evenly browned and fork inserted in center comes out clean.

Tivoli Fest Æbleskiver

Tivoli is the name of a large, famous amusement park in Copenhagen.

12 cups flour
1-1/2 cups sugar
1 tablespoon salt
1/2 cup baking powder

2 tablespoons baking soda
24 eggs, separated
3 quarts buttermilk

Mix flour, sugar, salt, baking powder, and baking soda. Add egg yolks and buttermilk. Whip egg whites and fold in last. Fill æbleskiver pan cups 1/4 full with Mazola oil before filling with batter. Fry until golden brown, turning often.

Note: This quantity is for a large crowd; it can be halved for a not-so-large crowd.

Coffee Cakes

Sweet Breads

Pastries

Danish Yeast Coffee Cake (Kaffekage)

2 cups milk, divided
1 package dry yeast
4 cups flour, divided
1/2 cup melted butter
1/2 cup sugar

1/2 lemon rind, grated
3 eggs, beaten
1 teaspoon cinnamon
2 tablespoons chopped almonds
2 tablespoons firm butter

Scald milk; cool to lukewarm. Pour 1/4 cup over yeast and let stand. Beat remaining milk into 2-1/4 cups of flour. Stir in yeast mixture; let rise until dough springs back to touch, then mix in melted butter, sugar, lemon rind, and eggs. Stir in remaining flour. Spread dough about 1 inch thick on two greased baking sheets and let rise again. When well risen, sprinkle with the cinnamon and almonds; dot with butter. Bake in preheated 400° oven for 15 minutes; lower heat to 375° and bake until brown (12 to 15 minutes).

Holiday Bread

1 cup sugar
1/2 cup butter
1 teaspoon salt
2 cups milk, scalded
2 packages dry yeast
1/4 cup warm milk
2 eggs
7-1/2 cups sifted flour, divided
2-1/2 cups candied fruit, divided

1 cup raisins
1 teaspoon cardamom
Melted butter

Topping:
1-1/2 cups powdered sugar
2 tablespoons very warm cream
1/4 teaspoon vanilla
Candied fruit (optional)

Mix together sugar, butter, salt, and scalded milk in a large bowl until butter is melted. Let stand to cool. Add yeast to the 1/4 cup warm milk, stir until dissolved, then add to the butter and milk mixture. Beat in eggs one at a time. Add 5 cups of flour a little at a time, beating after each addition. Coat 2 cups of the candied fruit, the raisins, and cardamom seeds with 1/2 cup of flour. Stir into basic mixture. Spread remaining flour on a board and knead the dough until smooth. Place dough in a greased bowl, brush with melted butter, cover, and let rise in a warm place until doubled. Put risen dough on board, punch down, and divide into three portions. Shape into loaves and place in greased 9x5x3-inch loaf pans. Let rise again until doubled. Bake in a preheated 450° oven for 10 minutes, then lower heat to 350° and bake 45 minutes or until lightly browned on top. Remove from oven and cool on a rack. Makes 3 loaves.

Topping: Mix all ingredients together and spread over tops of cooled bread, letting a little run over sides. Decorate with candied fruits if desired.

Anise-Almond Bread

2-1/4 cups sifted flour
2 teaspoons baking powder
1/2 teaspoon salt
1/2 cup soft butter
1 cup sugar

1 teaspoon anise seed
1/2 teaspoon almond extract
5 eggs
3/4 cup chopped, toasted almonds

Sift together the sifted flour, baking powder, and salt. Cream the butter and sugar; add the anise seed and almond extract and blend well. Beat in eggs one at a time, beating well after each addition. Mix in the dry ingredients thoroughly. Gently fold in chopped almonds. Pour batter into a greased, lightly floured 9x5x3-inch loaf pan. Bake in a preheated 350° oven for 1 hour. Makes 1 loaf.

Almond-Prune Bread

2 cups flour
2 teaspoons baking powder
1/2 teaspoon baking soda
1/2 teaspoon salt
3/4 cup sugar
1 tablespoon grated orange rind

3/4 cup chopped almonds
1 cup cooked, pitted, chopped prunes
2 eggs
1/4 cup prune juice
1/3 cup orange juice
1/4 cup melted butter

Sift together dry ingredients. Stir in orange rind, almonds, and prunes. Beat eggs until frothy and add to the dry mixture along with the prune and orange juice. Beat until well blended, then stir in butter and mix well. Place batter into greased, lightly floured 9x3x5-inch baking pan. Bake in preheated 350° oven 1 hour. Let cool on a rack. A thin glaze may be used to decorate the top. Makes 1 loaf.

Buttermilk-Nut Loaf

2-1/2 teaspoons baking powder
1 teaspoon baking soda
1/2 teaspoon salt
1/2 teaspoon cinnamon
1/4 teaspoon nutmeg
3/4 cup white flour

1-1/2 cups whole-wheat flour
3/4 cup brown sugar
1 egg
1-1/2 cups buttermilk
1 tablespoon melted butter
3/4 cup chopped nut meats

Sift together baking powder, soda, salt, cinnamon, nutmeg, and white flour. Add the whole-wheat flour and sift again. Add the brown sugar. Beat egg until light; mix in the buttermilk and melted butter and add to dry mixture. Stir in the nuts. Pour into a buttered and lightly floured 9x5x3-inch loaf pan. Bake in 325° pre-heated oven for 1 hour. Makes 1 loaf.

Danish Cones (Kræmmerhuse)

1/2 cup softened butter
1/2 cup sugar
1 cup sifted flour

5 egg whites, stiffly beaten
Whipped cream to taste

Cream the butter and sugar together until well blended. Add the flour and fold in stiffly beaten egg whites. Spread dough in a buttered 9x13-inch pan and bake in preheated 350° oven until light brown, about 30 minutes. Cut into squares while still warm and form each square into a cone shape. Cool, and just before serving, fill cones with whipped cream, flavored and sweetened to taste.

Note: If you do not have a cone form, form the cones by using the end of a wooden spoon or another utensil with a narrow end.

Shortbread

1-1/2 cups butter

3/4 cup + 2 tablespoons sugar, divided

1 egg

4 cups flour

1/2 cup chopped almonds

Cream together the butter and 3/4 cup of sugar. Beat in egg, then add enough flour to form a soft dough. On a lightly floured board, roll dough into a square about 1/3 inch thick. Cut into strips about 5/8 inches wide and 2 inches long. Sprinkle with the chopped almonds and remaining sugar. Place on a cookie sheet and bake in preheated 425° oven for 8 to 10 minutes.

Filled Pastries

3/4 cup butter

2-1/2 cups + 2 tablespoons sifted
   all-purpose flour, divided

1 package dry or compressed yeast

1/4 cup lukewarm water

2 tablespoons sugar

1/4 teaspoon salt

1/2 cup milk

1 egg + 1 egg yolk, lightly beaten

1/4 teaspoon vanilla extract or almond
   extract as desired

1/2 teaspoon grated lemon rind

1/2 teaspoon mace or nutmeg
   as desired

Filling:

Jam or cooked fruit of choice

Seasoning of choice

Small amount of cream

Cream together the butter and the 2 tablespoons of flour; shape into a ball and cool in the refrigerator. Dissolve yeast in the water. Combine the sugar, salt, and milk; add the lightly beaten egg plus yolk. Stir in the flavorings and gradually add

continued

milk; add the lightly beaten egg plus yolk. Stir in the flavorings and gradually add the remaining flour to form a pliable dough. On a lightly floured board, knead the dough until smooth. Place in a buttered bowl; cover with a towel and let rise in a warm place until doubled in size. Roll out dough approximately 1/3 inch thick; dot evenly with 1/4 of the cooled butter-flour mixture, leaving about 1-1/2 inches of edge unbuttered. Fold the dough in half and seal the edges. Pat dough lightly with hands and roll out again to about 1/3 inch thickness. Fold in half and let rest in a cool place for 10 minutes. Repeat this procedure two more times: rolling, dotting with butter-flour mixture, folding, and letting rest. Cut pastry into rounds, squares, or triangles. **Filling:** Mix all ingredients until creamy. Place a heaping teaspoonful of filling on each cut pastry; fold over. Lightly press edges together, leaving a little of the filling showing. Brush with egg wash (optional) and bake in preheated 450° oven for 15 to 18 minutes until lightly browned.

Cream Puffs

1 cup hot water
1/2 cup butter
1 cup flour

4 eggs
Filling of choice

Bring water and butter to boiling point in a large pan; add sifted flour. Stir vigorously until smooth and batter does not stick to spoon or sides of the pan. Cool slightly. Add eggs one at a time, beating well after each addition. Drop heaping spoonsful (teaspoon for smaller, tablespoon for larger) onto buttered baking sheet. Bake in 400° oven for about 10 minutes until puffed, then reduce heat to 350° and bake for 25 minutes longer. Puffs should be lightly browned and firm to the touch. Cool and fill with whipped cream, custard, or other filling of choice.

Danish Kringle

Pastry:
3/4 cup butter
2-3/4 to 3 cups sifted flour, divided
1 package dry yeast
1/4 cup lukewarm water
3 tablespoons sugar, divided
1 egg, beaten, divided
3/4 cup cold milk
1 teaspoon salt

Almond Filling:
1/4 cup butter
1-1/2 cups powdered sugar
1/2 teaspoon ground cardamom
1/4 cup finely chopped almonds
2 to 3 teaspoons heavy cream

(You may use any filling of choice:
pecan, cherry, apple, raisin, etc.)

Blend the butter and 1/4 cup of the flour together and set aside. Dissolve yeast in the lukewarm water, add 1 tablespoon sugar, and let stand 5 minutes. Beat together the egg (reserve 1 tablespoon for topping), cold milk, 2 tablespoons sugar, salt, and the yeast mixture. Blend in 2-1/2 to 3 cups flour to form a stiff dough. Chill in refrigerator for about 45 minutes, then, on a lightly floured surface, roll out to a 12-inch square. Roll the flour/butter mixture between sheets of waxed paper to a 10x4-inch rectangle and place in center of the dough. Fold each side of dough over flour/butter mixture; turn slightly and roll out again to a 12-inch square. Repeat the folding and rolling process two more times. Wrap the dough in waxed paper and chill for 30 to 60 minutes.

To prepare filling: Blend all ingredients together, using enough cream to form a spreading consistency.

continued

Danish Kringle *continued*

Assembly: Roll out chilled dough to a 24x12-inch rectangle, then cut lengthwise into two 24x6-inch strips. Spread each strip with filling and roll as a jelly roll, starting with the 24-inch edge. Moisten edges, seal, and stretch to about 30 inches. Place on greased baking sheet; shape into an oval or pretzel shape. Flatten to about 1/2-inch thickness. Brush with the reserved egg, cover with a moist cloth, and let rise in a warm place for 25 to 30 minutes. Bake in a preheated 375° oven for 25 to 30 minutes until golden brown. Makes 2.

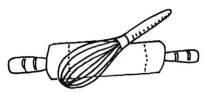

Breads, Rolls, Rusks

Danish Rye Bread

4 tablespoons sugar
4 tablespoons lard
4 cups hot water
1 cake compressed yeast

4 teaspoons salt
4 cups rye flour
White flour

Dissolve sugar and shortening in hot water; when lukewarm add the yeast and stir thoroughly. Add salt and rye flour to liquid mixture. Add enough white flour to make a stiff dough. Dough will be sticky. Knead slightly on a lightly floured surface; shape into four loaves. Place loaves in lightly greased loaf pans and let rise for about 3 hours. Bake at 350° for 1 hour.

Basic recipe from Mina Larsen, Danish Windmill, Elk Horn, Iowa

Danish Pumpernickel

1 cake compressed yeast
1/4 cup lukewarm water
1 quart buttermilk

3 teaspoons salt
8 cups rye flour
4 to 5 cups white flour

Dissolve yeast in the warm water. Heat buttermilk to lukewarm, then combine with the salt, rye flour, and yeast. Stir together thoroughly. Let stand overnight in a warm place. Next day, knead in enough white flour to make dough pliable and nonsticky. Shape into loaves, grease tops, and let rise until bulk is increased by about 1/3. Bake at 400° for 45 minutes; reduce heat to 300° and bake 2 hours more.

Black Bread

2 packages dry yeast	10 cups dark rye flour
1 teaspoon sugar	8 cups white all-purpose flour
1 tablespoon lukewarm water	1 tablespoon caraway seed
4-1/2 cups cold water	1 tablespoon melted butter
1-1/2 teaspoons salt	

Dissolve the yeast and sugar in the lukewarm water. Add the cold water, salt, flours, and caraway seed, mixing thoroughly to form a stiff dough. Knead on a lightly floured surface and let rise in a warm place until doubled. Punch down and knead again. Shape into loaves of desired size, place in lightly greased baking pans, and let rise again until doubled. Bake in preheated 425° oven for 10 minutes, reduce temperature to 350°, and bake about 1 hour. Brush tops with melted butter while still warm.

Danish Sourdough Bread
(Rugbrød med Surdej)

Step 1:
6-1/3 cups warm water
3 cups bread wheat flour
2 cups cracked rye seed
4 cups stone-ground rye flour
5 teaspoons salt
3/4 cup sourdough starter

Step 2:
2 cups bread wheat flour
2 cups stone-ground rye flour
1 cup warm water

Step 1: Combine first five ingredients; add sourdough starter. Let stand 8 hours.

continued

Danish Sourdough Bread *continued*

Step 2: Mixture should be a spongy consistency. Add the wheat and rye flours and warm water; knead in gently. (Reserve 3/4 cup of this dough for the next batch, which can be stored in the refrigerator for 8 to 14 days.) Fill two or three large or five medium-sized lightly oiled bread pans. Let rise 3 to 4 hours, but do not let dough double in bulk. Brush tops with vegetable oil or melted butter. Bake at 300° to 350° for 1-3/4 hours. Cool on racks.

—*Gerda Wallace, Kansas City, Missouri*

Dill or Caraway Bread

1 package dry yeast
1/4 cup warm water
1 cup small curd cottage cheese
2 tablespoons sugar
1 tablespoon minced onion
1 tablespoon melted butter

2 tablespoons dill or caraway seeds
1 teaspoon salt
1/4 teaspoon soda
1 unbeaten egg
2-1/4 to 2-1/2 cups all-purpose flour

Soften yeast in the warm water. Heat cottage cheese to warm; stir in sugar, onion, butter, dill or caraway seeds, salt, soda, and egg. Add the yeast and mix well. Add enough flour to make a stiff dough. Let rise in a warm place until doubled. Punch down and shape into two loaves. Put loaves into two well-greased baking pans and let rise again until doubled. Bake at 350° for about 1 hour.

Old-fashioned Clove Bread

2 tablespoons dry yeast
2 cups lukewarm milk
2 teaspoons salt
1/3 cup maple syrup
4 tablespoons vegetable oil
2 teaspoons ground cloves

2 teaspoons ground ginger
4-1/2 to 5 cups whole-wheat flour
(may use half unbleached white
flour)
Milk for brushing top
Poppy seeds for sprinkling on top

Dissolve the yeast in the warm milk. Mix in remaining ingredients, adding enough flour to make a stiff dough. Knead on lightly floured surface and let rise in a warm place for about 15 minutes. Divide dough into two parts and shape into 20-inch lengths. Twist the long rolls together and let rise about 20 minutes. Brush the tops with milk and sprinkle with poppy seeds. Bake on greased baking sheet at 375° for about 45 minutes.

Drop Biscuits

3 cups flour
1/2 teaspoon salt
2 tablespoons baking powder

2 tablespoons softened butter
1-1/2 cups milk

Sift together the flour, salt, and baking powder. Cut in the butter and work to form crumbs. Add the milk and beat to form a soft dough. Drop by heaping tablespoonsful about 1 inch apart on a greased baking sheet. Bake at 450° for 12 to 15 minutes.

Everyday Buns

2 packages dry yeast
1 cup lukewarm scalded milk
1/4 cup sugar
2 eggs, unbeaten

1 teaspoon salt
1/4 cup softened butter
4-3/4 cups all-purpose flour

Dissolve yeast in the lukewarm milk. Mix in the sugar, eggs, salt, and butter; mix thoroughly. Add flour gradually to form a smooth, pliable dough. Knead dough on a lightly floured surface, then let rise in a greased bowl until doubled in size. Work down; cut portions and shape into twelve buns. Place on greased cookie sheet or pan. Let rise again. Bake at 350° for 15 minutes until golden brown.

Lenten Rolls (Fastelavnsboller)

1 package dry yeast
1/4 cup lukewarm water
1-1/2 cups scalded milk
1/2 cup butter or margarine
1/3 cup sugar
1 teaspoon salt

2 eggs, beaten
4-1/2 cups flour, divided
1 cup raisins
1/3 cup chopped citron
1/2 teaspoon cardamom
1 tablespoon melted butter

Dissolve yeast in the warm water. Mix together scalded milk, butter, sugar, and salt; add eggs, yeast, and 2 cups of the flour. Beat until bubbly. Stir in raisins, citron, cardamom, and remaining flour. Knead well on a lightly floured surface. Place in a greased bowl and let rise until doubled. Shape into small balls. Place on a greased cookie sheet; let rise again until light. Brush tops with melted butter. Bake at 375° for 15 to 20 minutes. Drizzle with a powdered sugar glaze.

Rusks (Zweibak)

2-1/2 cups flour
1 teaspoon baking powder
1/2 cup butter
1/4 cup sugar

1 egg
1/2 teaspoon salt
3/4 cup milk
1 teaspoon cardamom

Sift flour and baking powder together into a bowl. Cut in butter and sugar until well blended. Beat in egg, salt, and milk. Add cardamom. Mix well to form a smooth dough. Form into small balls and place on a greased baking sheet. Bake at 375° for 15 minutes. Let cool, then split in half. Dry in a slow oven (about 200°) until crisp and golden brown. Store in an airtight container.

Fancy Almond Rusks

1 cup brown sugar
2 eggs, beaten
7 tablespoons softened butter
2-1/2 to 3 tablespoons slivered
   almonds

3 cups flour
1 teaspoon baking powder
Salt to taste

Beat sugar and eggs together until light. Cream the butter and add to the egg mixture. Stir in almonds. Sift flour, baking powder, and salt together and add a little at a time to egg mixture, beating well after each addition. Spread the dough about 1 1/2 inches thick on a buttered baking sheet. Bake at 375° for 15 minutes. Remove from baking sheet and cut diagonally into 3/4-inch-thick pieces. Dry in a slow oven if a crispier texture is desired.

mørrebrød

(Danish Open-Faced Sandwiches)

Bread and Butter and More

Plenty of butter, cream, and a hearty bread are essential to the Danish cook. Daily meals may be plain and thrifty, but they are always nicely garnished and presented with an elegance fit for a king. Smørrebrød, open-faced sandwiches, are a famous feature of the Danish kitchen. The word smørrebrød literally means "buttered bread," but the bread itself is largely downstaged by a blend of flavors, texture, and color achieved by the "creator" of this staple in a Dane's diet. Open-faced sandwiches are eaten—always with a knife and fork—as a first course, as a lunch, even as a full-course meal. Because of the wide variety and choice of ingredients, the open-faced sandwich never loses its appeal. The creator, often the consumer, is limited only by one's own imagination. Some of the more popular ingredients and tastes are listed on the following pages.

Suggested Basics to Begin

Thin slices of buttered bread

Hard-cooked or scrambled eggs

Pickled or smoked herring

Liver paste

Shrimp

Lobster

Smoked eel

Sardines

Smoked salmon

Oysters

Crab

Warm fish fillets (sole, flounder, etc.)

Frikadeller (meatballs)

Sliced ham

Rolled veal

Sliced tongue

Pressed lamb

Sliced beef and/or pork

Bacon

Salami

Chicken spreads

Roast duck

Assorted cheeses (Danish Blue, Camembert, Swiss, etc.)

Suggested Garnishes to Finish

Radish slices
Pickled beets
Tomato slices
Cucumber slices (usually marinated)
Onion rings (raw or fried)
Parsley, dill, chives, or watercress
Lettuce
Spinach
Red cabbage salad
Jellied consommé
Anchovies
Caviar

Pickles
Olives
Mushrooms (raw or fried)
Remoulade
Mayonnaise
Tartar sauce
Relishes (pickle, beet, etc.)
Jellies
Fresh fruit
Curry salad
Herring salad
Italian salad

Some Favored Combinations

- Swiss cheese with radishes. Butter white or rye bread and place two to three slices of cheese on top. Cover with sliced radishes. Garnish with parsley, lettuce leaf, and radish cut as a flower.
- Shrimp. This sandwich is best on white bread. Pile freshly cooked, peeled shrimp on generously buttered bread. Garnish with a lemon twist and lettuce.
- Roast pork with pickled beets and red cabbage. Place slices of roast pork on thickly buttered bread; garnish with twists of pickled beets and red cabbage.
- Egg with herring tidbits. Put slices of hard-cooked egg on top of thickly buttered pumpernickel. Garnish with pickled herring and/or anchovies as desired.

Cucumbers in Sour Cream

1 tablespoon + 1 teaspoon salt
3 medium-sized cucumbers, sliced thin
1 medium-sized onion, sliced thin
1/2 cup sour cream
1 tablespoon sugar

1 tablespoon lemon juice
Dash of pepper
1 teaspoon sesame seeds (optional)

Mix 1 tablespoon of the salt with cucumber and onion slices; set aside for 15 to 20 minutes. Mix together remaining ingredients. Rinse the salted cucumber and onion in clear water; press out liquid. Stir in the sour cream mixture. Chill before serving.

Cucumber Salad (Agurkesalat)

3 cucumbers
1 tablespoon salt
1/2 cup vinegar
1/2 cup sugar

1-1/2 cups water
1/4 teaspoon pepper
Parsley for garnish

Wash cucumbers; slice thinly. Sprinkle with the salt and let sit for about 2 hours to draw out bitterness. Rinse and drain thoroughly. Mix the vinegar, sugar, water, and pepper together until sugar is dissolved. Pour over the cucumbers and chill. Garnish with snipped parsley.

Curry Salad

Curry Dressing:
1 cup unsweetened whipped cream
1/2 cup mayonnaise
1-1/2 teaspoons curry powder
1/8 teaspoon salt
1/8 teaspoon white pepper
1 teaspoon white wine vinegar
Salad:

2 hard-cooked eggs
16 ounces marinated herring, chopped
1 cup diced ham
1/2 cup diced cucumber
2 cups cooked rice
Lettuce leaves
Fennel for garnish

Dressing: Fold all ingredients into the whipped cream. **Salad:** Place all salad ingredients, except lettuce and fennel, into a large bowl. Pour dressing over all and toss gently. Chill. Serve on crisp lettuce leaf; sprinkle with fennel. Serves 6.

Herring Salad

Salad Dressing:
1/4 cup vinegar
2 tablespoons water or beet juice
2 tablespoons sugar
Dash of white pepper
Salad:
2 fillets salt herring, diced

1-1/2 cups diced boiled potatoes
1-1/2 cups pickled beets
1/3 cup diced dill pickle
1/2 cup diced apple
1/4 cup finely chopped onion
2 hard-cooked eggs for garnish
Chopped fresh parsley for garnish

Dressing: Blend together the vinegar, water, sugar, and pepper. **Salad:** Place all salad ingredients in a large bowl; add dressing, stirring gently. Pack into a lightly oiled 5-cup mold; chill for a few hours. Unmold and garnish with hard-cooked eggs and parsley. Serves 4 to 6.

Red Cabbage Salad

Salad Dressing:
1 cup whipping cream
Juice of 1 lemon
Salt to taste
1 tablespoon sugar

Salad:
1 medium-sized head red cabbage
1 large tart apple, pared and diced
3 ribs celery, cut into short pieces

Dressing: Mix all dressing ingredients together and chill. **Salad:** Remove outer leaves of cabbage; core and shred, but not too fine. Mix in the apple and celery. Stir in the dressing and chill until serving time. Serves 6.

Hot Potato Salad

1 large onion, cut into chunks

2 tablespoons butter

1/2 teaspoon salt

1 teaspoon sugar

3 tablespoons vinegar

8 medium-sized pared, boiled potatoes

2 tablespoons heavy cream

Dash of pepper

Boil the onion in a small amount of water; add butter, salt, sugar, and vinegar and cook until onion is tender. Slice potatoes and add to the onion. Warm mixture slowly; stir gently, being careful not to break the potatoes. Add the cream and pepper. Serve hot with cold meats. Serves 8 to 10.

Soups

Barley Soup

3/4 cup pearl barley
3 pints beef stock, divided
1 onion, chopped
3 carrots, diced
1/2 cup chopped celery

3/4 cup chopped mushrooms
3 tablespoons butter
1 teaspoon salt
1/2 teaspoon white pepper
1/4 cup sour cream

Cook the barley on low heat in half the stock for about 1 hour. Boil the onion, carrots, celery, and mushrooms in remaining stock until tender; combine with the barley mixture. Add the butter, salt, and pepper and continue to simmer for a few minutes. Remove from heat and blend in the sour cream. Serve hot or cold. Serves 4 to 6.

Beet Soup

12 large beets
2 pounds short ribs
1/2 cup lemon juice
1/3 cup sugar
1 teaspoon allspice

1 onion, sliced
Salt to taste
White pepper to taste
Sour cream for topping

Scrub and scrape the beets; do not peel. Cut beets into chunks. Place remaining ingredients, except sour cream, into a large kettle; cover with water and bring to a boil. Cover, reduce heat, and simmer for about 2-1/2 hours. When done, strain through a sieve or colander. (Reserve the short ribs for leftover use.) Chill and serve cold with a dollop of sour cream. Serves 6.

Danish Vegetable Soup with Dumplings

1 large beef bone or knuckle
Water to cover
3 teaspoons salt, divided
1/4 teaspoon pepper
3 large onions, chopped
4 large carrots, sliced 1/2 inch thick

6 or 8 potatoes, whole and peeled
1 egg, lightly beaten
Flour
1/2 teaspoon baking powder
Fresh parsley leaves, chopped

Place beef bone in a soup kettle; cover with water and add 2 teaspoons salt. Bring to a boil and cook until meat falls off the bone. Remove bone from broth; remove meat from bone, chop, and return to broth. Add the pepper, onions, carrots, and whole potatoes; bring to a boil and simmer until vegetables are tender. Remove

continued

potatoes; mash and add 1 teaspoon salt, the egg, enough flour to make a ball of dough that leaves sides of pan, and baking powder. Dip a spoon in the boiling broth and cut off dough to make dumplings. Drop pieces of the dough into the boiling broth; cover and cook for 5 minutes. Turn dumplings and cook 5 minutes more. Serve hot, garnished with fresh parsley. Serves 6 to 8.

Green Kale Soup (Grønkaalssuppe)

4 to 5 pounds pork ribs or ham
    with bone
1 beef bone
2 leeks or onions
1 tablespoon salt
Soup swag of celery and parsley

1/2 cup barley
3 medium-sized potatoes, diced
3 large carrots, diced
3 cups kale, hard spine removed,
    washed, and chopped in a food
    grinder

Cover meat and beef bone with water; bring to a boil and cook on low for 1-1/4 hours. Skim as necessary. Add leeks or onions, salt, and celery and parsley tied in a swag. When meat is tender, remove to a platter. Strain broth; return to kettle and add barley, diced potatoes, and carrots; cook until almost tender. Add the kale about 20 to 30 minutes before other vegetables are fully cooked.

Buttermilk Soup (Kærnemælksuppe)

3 tablespoons flour
6 cups buttermilk, divided
1/2 cup sugar
1/2 cup raisins

1/2 lemon rind, grated
1 cinnamon stick
Whipped cream (optional)

Mix flour with 1/2 cup of the buttermilk to make a paste. Slowly add remaining buttermilk and heat slowly. Add the sugar, raisins, grated lemon rind, and cinnamon stick. Cook slowly, stirring constantly, until raisins are soft and plump. Remove cinnamon stick and serve hot with a dollop of whipped cream on top if desired. Serves 4 to 6.

Holiday Fruit Soup (Sødsuppe)

8 cups water
1 cup sugar
1/2 teaspoon salt
1/2 cup sago or cornstarch
1 cup pitted prunes
1 cup raisins

1/2 seedless orange, peeled and diced
1/2 lemon, peeled and diced
3 apples, cored, pared, and diced
3 peaches, pared, pitted, and diced
1/2 cup tapioca
2 cinnamon sticks

Bring water to a boil; add sugar and salt. Make a paste of the sago and a little water; stir into boiling mixture. Add fruits, tapioca, and cinnamon sticks and boil slowly for about 1 hour. Remove cinnamon sticks. Serve hot or cold with croutons. Serves 8.

Rhubarb Soup with Wine

1 tablespoon cornstarch
3/4 cup sugar
1 cup water
1/2 teaspoon ground cinnamon
1/2 teaspoon nutmeg

3 slices of lemon
2 cups red wine
3 cups chopped fresh rhubarb
2 sticks cinnamon
Whipped cream (optional)

Dissolve the cornstarch and sugar in the water; heat, stirring continually, until mixture reaches boiling point. Add the spices, lemon slices, wine, rhubarb, and cinnamon sticks. Cook for 5 minutes or until rhubarb is tender. Remove cinnamon sticks and serve hot or cold. Top with whipped cream if desired. Serves 4.

Cherry Soup (Kirsebærsuppe)

1-1/2 pounds cherries, divided
3 quarts water
1 cinnamon stick

1/2 lemon, sliced
2 tablespoons cornstarch
1/2 cup sugar

Pit 1 cup of the cherries and reserve. Cook remaining cherries in the 3 quarts of water; when tender, press through a sieve. Add the cup of pitted cherries, cinnamon stick, and lemon slices to the juice. Cook slowly for a few minutes. Make a paste of cornstarch and a little juice, and add to the soup. Bring to a boil and add the sugar. Serve hot or cold. Serves 8.

Main Dishes

(Meats, Poultry, Game, Fish)

Roast Pork with Prunes

4 to 5 pound pork loin
16 prunes, halved and pitted
2 teaspoons salt
1 teaspoon pepper
1/4 teaspoon ginger (optional)

3 tablespoons flour
1/4 cup prune juice
2-3/4 cups water
Salt and pepper to taste
1 teaspoon red currant jelly

(Flaskesteg med Svesker)

Cut deep slits in pork loin and insert prune halves. Rub with the salt, pepper, and ginger (if desired). Roast uncovered in a 325° oven for about 1-1/2 hours. When done, remove from roasting pan. Heat pan drippings; stir in the flour, then add the prune juice and water. Season and cook until thickened. Stir in the jelly and serve the gravy over the sliced pork. Serves 8 to 10.

Pork Sausages (Medisterpølser)

4 pounds lean pork
1 pound side pork
1/2 teaspoon each allspice and ground
    cloves
1 tablespoon salt

1 teaspoon pepper
1 large onion, grated
1 cup stock
1 tablespoon butter or margarine
2 tablespoons flour

Grind meats together three to five times. Add seasonings and onion; mix well, adding stock a little at a time. Stuff into small (lamb, pork, or small beef) casings, not too firmly. Place sausages in a frying pan and cover with boiling water; bring to a boil. Remove sausages from broth. Save broth for gravy. Melt butter or margarine in a pan and brown sausages on both sides. Remove sausages and mix flour with fat in pan; add the broth and cook until thickened.

Rolled Veal (Rullepølse)

1 flank of veal
1 teaspoon salt
1/2 teaspoon pepper
1/2 teaspoon ground allspice
1 teaspoon saltpeter*
4 slices bacon

Brine:
1 cup salt
4 bay leaves
1/2 teaspoon saltpeter
2 quarts boiling water

Remove sinews from veal. Flatten meat on a board and rub in the seasonings and saltpeter. Put bacon on top. Roll meat tightly and tie. Place in a ceramic or glass container.

continued

Brine: Mix salt, bay leaves, and saltpeter in the boiling water; cool and pour over the meat. After 5 or 6 days, remove the meat from the brine, cover with boiling salted water, and cook slowly for about 2-1/2 hours. Remove meat from the stock and place between two flat surfaces with a weight on top. When cold, slice very thin for open-faced sandwiches. The broth makes a good base for vegetable soup.

*Saltpeter can be found at a pharmacy or butcher shop.

Liver Paste (Leverpostej)

1-1/2 pounds liver (pork, calf, or chicken)
1 large onion, minced
5 anchovies (optional)
4 tablespoons butter
2 tablespoons flour
1 cup milk
1-1/2 teaspoons salt
1/2 teaspoon pepper
1/2 teaspoon allspice
2 eggs
1 strip of bacon

Grind liver, onion, and anchovies together thoroughly; set aside. Melt butter in a saucepan, add flour, and mix until smooth. Add milk a little at a time, stirring until thickened. Cool to lukewarm; add spices and eggs. Mix sauce with the liver mixture. Place strip of bacon in bottom of a loaf pan before adding liver mixture. Place pan in a larger pan with hot water and bake about 1 hour in a 350° oven.

Danish Stew with Dumplings

Stew:
3 tablespoons butter
2 onions, chopped
3 tablespoons flour
2 cups beef stock
3 pounds round steak, cut in chunks
3 tablespoons vinegar
1 teaspoon salt
1/2 teaspoon white pepper

Dumplings:
3/4 cup flour
3/4 teaspoon baking powder
1/2 teaspoon salt
1 tablespoon minced parsley
1/4 teaspoon marjoram
3 tablespoons butter
2 tablespoons ice water

Melt butter over low heat, add onions, and brown. Stir in 3 tablespoons of flour until smooth. Add stock slowly, stirring until mixture boils and thickens. Set aside. Place meat in a heavy skillet and sprinkle with the vinegar. Add the sauce, teaspoon of salt, and pepper and mix well. Cover and cook over low heat for 2 hours.

To prepare dumplings: Sift flour, baking powder, and 1/2 teaspoon salt in a bowl. Add parsley and marjoram; mix well. Cut in the butter, add ice water, and toss lightly until a ball of dough is formed. Shape dough into small balls and drop into the stew; continue to cook over low heat 35 minutes more. Serves 6 to 8.

Danish Meatballs & Brown Gravy
(Frikadeller)

Meatballs:
1-1/2 pounds ground round steak
1/2 pound ground pork
1 onion, diced
1/2 cup bread or cracker crumbs
1-1/2 teaspoons salt
Dash of pepper
2 tablespoons flour

2 eggs
1/2 cup milk
Shortening or bacon fat
Gravy:
3 tablespoons flour
3/4 tablespoon drippings
1-1/2 cups light cream or milk
Salt and pepper

Grind meats together three or four times. Mix in the diced onion, crumbs, salt, pepper, flour, and eggs. Add just enough milk to make a consistency for shaping

flour, and eggs. Add just enough milk to make a consistency for shaping balls. Fry the meatballs in shortening or bacon fat until browned on all sides. Cover and simmer slowly until cooked through.

To make gravy: Stir flour into drippings until browned. Slowly add the cream or milk, stirring constantly, until thickened. Season to taste. Gently mix gravy with the meatballs.

Birds (Benløse Fugle)

6 slices round steak	Pork sausage
Salt	6 strips fresh pork fat
Pepper	Parsley, minced (optional)
Ginger (optional)	Flour for dredging
Ground cloves (optional)	Fat for frying
1 medium-sized onion, minced	Water, meat stock, or cream

Cut steak into pieces of suitable size for rolling and serving after pounding. Flatten each piece and season to taste. Spread a thin layer of minced onion and sausage over each piece. Place a strip of pork fat in the center; sprinkle with parsley if desired. Roll up and secure with string or a toothpick. Dredge each "bird" in flour. Brown in hot fat. Add a little hot water, stock, or cream, and cook slowly until meat is tender. Remove from pan. Add a little flour to pan liquid to make a gravy to pour over birds to serve.

Variations: Chopped onion, celery, and tomato may be used as filler with a strip of bacon wrapped around the bird. In parts of Denmark, veal is used with parsley and a strip of pork fat as filler. Pork may also be used for birds and filled with pitted prunes.

Danish Meatballs (Frikadeller)

1-1/2 pounds ground round steak
1/2 pound ground pork
1 onion, grated
3 to 4 slices white bread
Milk
1/3 teaspoon pepper

1/4 cup flour
1/2 teaspoon cloves
1-1/2 teaspoons salt
2 eggs
Cream
1 tablespoon butter for frying

Grind meats together three or four times. Add grated onion. Soften bread in milk; add to meat mixture. Thoroughly mix in remaining ingredients, using just enough cream to make a smooth consistency for shaping small balls. Melt butter in a frying pan and brown meatballs on all sides.

Stuffed Spareribs

1 cup prunes

2 sides of spareribs (3 to 4 pounds)

Salt and pepper

4 apples

1 tablespoon flour

Soak prunes several hours or overnight. Cut in half and remove pits. Season sides of spareribs with salt and pepper. Pare and core apples; cut into eighths. Lay one side of spareribs in roasting pan and place prunes and apples over, then cover with other side. Tie with a cord. Sprinkle with the flour. Sear in preheated 400° oven for about 20 minutes. Reduce heat to 325°; cover and continue cooking for approximately 2-1/2 hours until fully cooked and tender.

Stuffed Cabbage Rolls
(Fyldte Hvidkaalshoved eller Rouletter)

1 large head white cabbage	Salt and pepper to taste
1 pound ground beef	3 tablespoons flour
1/2 pound ground pork	1/2 cup dry bread crumbs
1 large onion, minced	1 cup milk
1 egg	3 tablespoons butter

Place head of cabbage into a kettle of boiling water; blanch for about 5 minutes or until leaves are wilted. Drain and cool slightly. Remove leaves one at a time. Mix meats and remaining ingredients, except the butter, together. Place a heaping tablespoonful of the mixture in the center of each cabbage leaf. Fold stem part

of leaf over meat, fold in sides, and continue to roll up leaf. Fasten with toothpick or tie with string to hold. Melt the butter in a large, heavy skillet and brown the rolls. Add just enough water to cover; simmer for 30 minutes. Arrange rolls on a platter. Thicken the broth with enough flour to make a gravy. Pour gravy over rolls to serve. Serves 6 to 8.

Dana College, Blair, Nebraska
Photo courtesy Dana College

Danish Beef Stew

1/4 cup butter
Generous pinch of pepper
2-1/2 teaspoons salt, divided
2 pounds round steak, cut into cubes
4 medium-sized onions

2 cups boiling water
1 tablespoon brown sugar
6 small bay leaves
4 tablespoons flour
6 tablespoons cold water

Melt butter in a large skillet. Add pepper and 2 teaspoons of salt. Brown meat in the seasoned butter, about 10 minutes. Cut onions in half, lengthwise; slice paper-thin and sear with meat cubes for about 5 minutes. Add boiling water, brown sugar, 1/2 teaspoon salt, and bay leaves. Cover and bring to a boil; reduce heat and simmer 1 hour. Remove bay leaves. Mix flour and cold water to make a smooth paste; add to meat mixture and cook until thickened. Serves 6.

Roast with Beer

5 tablespoons flour, divided
4 teaspoons ginger
Salt and pepper to taste

4 pound roast (pork, beef, lamb, or veal)
12 ounces beer
3 tablespoons cold water

Mix 2 tablespoons of the flour with ginger, salt, and pepper. Rub into the roast. Roast in a preheated 475° oven for 10 minutes, then reduce heat to 325°. Pour beer over the roast; baste every 20 minutes until done (35 minutes per pound). Mix 3 tablespoons flour with cold water until smooth. Drain fat from pan juices; add flour mixture. Stir until thickened, about 4 minutes. Serve the gravy along with the sliced roast. Serves 8 to 10.

Roast Goose for Christmas
(Stegt Julegaas)

1 large goose (about 14 pounds)
1 teaspoon salt
White pepper to taste
1 tablespoon caraway seed
Stuffing:
2 tablespoons water

4 cups diced apples
2-1/2 cups dry bread crumbs
1 small onion, chopped
1 cup white wine
2 cups prunes, stoned

Several hours before roasting, wash goose thoroughly inside and out. Dry well.
Remove any remaining pin feathers. Using a sharp fork, prick skin to allow fat to

drain while cooking. Combine salt, pepper, and caraway seed; rub well into the skin and interior cavities.

To prepare stuffing: In a saucepan, add the water to the diced apples and cook until soft. Mash the apples; add the bread crumbs, chopped onion, and pepper. Mix well. Stuff the goose with apple mixture and fasten opening with a skewer. Place in a shallow pan and roast in preheated 350° oven for 3 hours; skim off fat as it accumulates. After goose has cooked for 3 hours, pour the wine over all; arrange prunes around goose and cook for 3 hours more, basting often. The skin should be brown and crisp when done. Serves 14.

Roast Duck with Danish Stuffing

1 duck (about 6 pounds), cleaned
   and dressed (reserve neck and
   giblets)
Salt to taste
1 small onion, minced
2 tablespoons butter

Pepper to taste
1 cup chopped celery
1-1/2 cups dry bread crumbs
1 cup cooked prune pulp
1 cup chopped tart apple
1/2 cup melted butter

Sprinkle inside of duck with salt. **Prepare the stuffing:** In a large skillet, brown the onion in 2 tablespoons butter. Remove from heat; add salt and pepper to taste, celery, and bread crumbs. Mix well. Add prune pulp, chopped apple, and melted butter. Stuff the duck and place on a rack in an open roasting pan. Roast in preheated 400° oven for 15 minutes. Reduce heat to 350° and continue to roast, allowing 25 minutes per pound. Cook neck and giblets until tender in water seasoned with salt and pepper. When tender, remove skin and bones from neck; chop meat and giblets finely and add to gravy if desired. Serves 8.

The Danish Windmill, left, Elk Horn, Iowa, was imported from Denmark. Solvang, California, has attractive replicas of Danish windmills.

Roast Leg of Venison

6 to 7 pound leg of venison
4 ounces salt pork fat for larding
1-1/2 teaspoons salt
1/4 teaspoon pepper
1/4 teaspoon ginger
2 tablespoons olive or vegetable oil
1 cup butter

2 cups beef stock or bouillon
Gravy:
Pan drippings
1/3 cup flour
2 tablespoons dry red wine
2 tablespoons currant jelly
1/4 teaspoon grated orange peel

Fresh venison should be hung in a cool place for four days or longer. Rinse meat and dry well. Remove all skin and sinews. Cut salt pork into strips about 1/3 inch wide and 2 inches long. Roll them in a mixture of the salt, pepper, and ginger.

Insert strips into the meat with a larding needle at evenly spaced intervals; leave both ends of the fat showing. (You might ask a butcher to do the larding.) Rub the meat with any remaining seasonings, then with the olive or vegetable oil. Melt butter in roaster and sear roast before placing in oven. Roast, uncovered, in a 350° oven for 2-1/2 to 3 hours, or until brown and tender. Baste often with the beef stock or bouillon. **To prepare gravy:** When the roast is tender and cooked through, remove to a platter and keep warm. Skim the fat from the pan drippings. Mix the flour with a little water and stir mixture into pan drippings; continue to stir, add the wine, and boil a few minutes. Stir in the currant jelly and orange peel and cook until thickened. Serve the gravy as a side with the sliced venison. Serves 12.

Roast Pheasant with Stuffing

2 pheasants, cleaned and dressed
Salt to taste
Pepper to taste
4 tablespoons butter
2 cups white wine

Stuffing:
1/4 cup butter
1/4 cup heavy cream
4 cups bread crumbs
Salt to taste
Pepper to taste
3 egg yolks

Split each pheasant down the back into halves; salt and pepper to taste. Melt the butter in a large heavy skillet and brown the pheasant halves on both sides. **Prepare the stuffing:** Heat the butter and cream just to boiling point; stir in bread

crumbs and salt and pepper to taste. Beat in the egg yolks. Place stuffing in each half and arrange in a roasting pan; pour the wine over all and roast, covered, in a preheated 350° oven for 2-1/2 to 3 hours (until brown and tender). Baste with pan drippings during roasting. If more browning is desired, remove cover for last 20 minutes of roasting. Serves 6 to 8.

The Morning Star Chapel, near the Danish Immigrant Museum in Elk Horn, Iowa, was built by an 83-year-old Iowan, Charles Walensky, a Danish immigrant to Waterloo.

Boiled Fish

1-1/2-inch-thick slices of large fish
   (cod, salmon, halibut, mackerel)
Salt as needed

Boiling water: 1 tablespoon salt
   + 2 tablespoons vinegar per
   1 quart water

Rinse fish slices in cold running water. Sprinkle generously with salt and leave for 15 minutes. Rinse again, then place in boiling water to which 1 tablespoon of salt and 2 tablespoons of vinegar per quart of water have been added. Cover and slowly bring back to a boil. Turn off heat and let fish steam with a tightly closed lid for about 10 minutes. Remove fish carefully from water; place on a rack to drain before serving with a sauce of choice.

Note: To prevent fish from breaking, tie a cloth around the fish or use a pan with a rack.

Fish Balls

2 cups salted codfish or other white fish
3 cups raw, diced potatoes
1 egg

2 tablespoons melted butter
Pepper to taste
1/8 teaspoon dry mustard
Hot fat for frying

Soak salted fish in cold water overnight. Drain and soak 1 hour more. Drain. Place fish and diced potatoes in a saucepan; cover with water and cook until potatoes are tender. Drain. Beat egg, butter, pepper, and dry mustard together. Add the fish and potato mixture and beat well. Drop tablespoonsful into hot fat and fry until golden brown. Drain on paper towels and serve with sauce of choice. Serves 4 to 5.

Fried Flounder with Cream

1 pound flounder fillets or other
    white fish
1/2 cup dry bread crumbs

3 tablespoons butter
2 medium-sized onions, thinly sliced
1/2 cup heavy cream

Dredge and coat fish fillets in bread crumbs. Melt butter in heavy skillet and sauté onions until golden brown. Remove onions from skillet; fry fish fillets in same skillet until flaky and golden brown. Place fish on a platter; cover with the onions. Pour cream into skillet and heat to almost a boil. Pour cream over the fish and onions. Serves 4.

Pickled Herring

4 pounds of cleaned and boned
    herring
1-1/2 quarts vinegar
3 quarts water

1 cup sugar
2 teaspoons pepper
1 teaspoon whole cloves
1/2 cup hops

Soak herring in a mixture of the vinegar and water for at least 24 hours. Drain, then place first layer in an earthenware crock or glass container. Mix together the sugar, pepper, cloves, and hops. Spread a layer of spice mixture over the layer of herring. Repeat layering; finish with layer of spice mixture. Place weight on top and allow to season in a cool place for about 2 weeks.

Note: A tightly sealed plastic bag filled with water is useful as a weight.

Fish Pudding

1 teaspoon salt
2-1/2 pounds ground fish (cod,
    halibut, or trout)

1-1/2 cups heavy cream, whipped
3 egg whites, beaten until stiff

Stir salt into ground fish. Fold whipped cream into fish; mix well. Fold in beaten egg whites. Pour into generously buttered mold, filling to about 3/4 full. Place mold in a pan of hot water. Cover and bake 1 hour in a 325° oven. Unmold on a hot serving platter and serve with sauce of choice. (**See Sauces.**)

Fish Cooked in Beer

1 whole cod, mackerel, or other
   fresh fish, cleaned and scaled if
   necessary
1 onion, sliced
Grated rind and juice of 1 lemon
3 tablespoons vinegar
1 tablespoon molasses

1/2 cup melted butter
3 bay leaves
1/2 teaspoon salt
1/2 teaspoon pepper
1 teaspoon paprika
1/2 cup dry bread crumbs
Beer

Place fish in a shallow baking pan. Spread sliced onion and grated lemon rind over the fish. Mix together the lemon juice, vinegar, molasses, butter, bay leaves, salt, pepper, and paprika. Pour over the fish. Sprinkle top with bread crumbs. Pour in enough beer to almost cover. Bake in a preheated 350° oven for about 40 minutes or until well browned.

Vegetables

Browned Small Potatoes
(Brunede Kartofler)

10 to 12 small potatoes
1 tablespoon butter

2 tablespoons sugar
Salt

Scrub potatoes; cover with lightly salted water and cook until tender. Melt butter in a skillet over moderate heat; stir in the sugar. Brown but do not burn. Add the potatoes. Turn potatoes until they are coated with the butter-sugar mixture. Continue to turn until potatoes are browned. Sprinkle a little salt over the browned potatoes and serve.

Sweet-Sour Red Cabbage (Rødkaal)

1 medium-sized onion, thinly sliced
2 tablespoons butter
1 cup water
4 cups shredded red cabbage
2 cups peeled, diced, tart apples

3 tablespoons white vinegar
1 tablespoon brown sugar
1/4 teaspoon ground allspice
2 whole cloves

In a large skillet, brown sliced onion in the butter. Stir in remaining ingredients in order listed. Bring to a boil; reduce heat and simmer until cabbage is almost tender. Serves 6 to 8.

Browned White Cabbage (Brunkaal)

1 medium-sized white cabbage   1/4 teaspoon salt
1 tablespoon butter   Water as needed
2 tablespoons sugar

Shred the cabbage; discard the core. Melt butter in a heavy skillet over moderate heat; stir in sugar until browned. Add the cabbage and stir until browned. Add salt and a little water. Cover and let simmer for about 2 hours. Stir occasionally, adding water as needed. Serves 6 to 8.

First-Harvest Vegetables

2 cups cubed new potatoes, cooked
1 cup sliced new carrots, cooked
1 cup fresh shelled peas, cooked
2 tablespoons butter
2 tablespoons flour

1 tablespoon minced green onion tops
2 cups milk
1 teaspoon salt
Dash of pepper

Set aside cooked vegetables. In a saucepan, melt butter; stir in flour and green onion tops until smooth. Slowly add milk, stirring constantly. Add seasonings and cooked vegetables. Simmer together for 15 minutes. Serves 6.

Note: Ham or bacon may be added, as well as other combinations of vegetables.

Creamed Kale (Grønlangskaal)

2 stalks kale
3 tablespoons butter
3 tablespoons flour

2 cups milk
1 teaspoon salt
1 tablespoon sugar

Soak kale in cold, lightly salted water to clean. Rinse and remove stalks and tough veins of the leaves. Put leaves in a saucepan with a tight-fitting lid. Add enough water to steam-cook leaves until tender. Drain and chop fine; set aside. Melt the butter and stir in flour until smooth. Slowly add milk and cook until thickened. Add the chopped kale to the thickened sauce. Season with the salt and sugar and heat thoroughly. Serves 4.

Green Beans with Mushrooms

1-1/2 pounds green beans
1/2 teaspoon sugar
1/4 teaspoon salt
1/4 teaspoon white pepper
1/2 pound mushrooms, sliced
2 tablespoons butter

2 tablespoons flour
1-1/2 cups light cream
Juice of 1 lemon
Dried bread crumbs
3/4 cup chopped almonds

Break off ends of beans. Add sugar, salt and pepper, and enough water to cover. Cook until tender. Drain. Sauté mushrooms in the butter until tender. Cool slightly. Stir in flour; slowly add cream, stirring constantly. Cook on low until thickened. Remove from heat; add lemon juice. Combine beans and sauce in a baking dish. Top with bread crumbs and almonds. Heat in a 350° oven for 20 to 30 minutes. Serves 8.

Sauces
&
Dressings
for
meats, fish, & vegetables

Chive Sauce

1/2 cup butter

3 egg yolks

2 tablespoons lemon juice

Salt to taste

1-1/2 tablespoons chopped chives

Melt butter in a saucepan; do not brown. Blend together egg yolks, lemon juice, and salt. Blend in melted butter and beat in chives. Makes 3/4 cup.

Sour Cream Sauce

1 cup sour cream

1 teaspoon prepared mustard

1 teaspoon prepared horseradish

Salt to taste

1/2 teaspoon sugar

Blend all ingredients together and let stand at room temperature for 1 hour.

Dill Sauce

1 cup mayonnaise
1 teaspoon dry mustard
1 tablespoon lemon juice

1/2 cup heavy cream, whipped
1 tablespoon dried dill or 1/2
    teaspoon fresh, minced dill weed

Blend together mayonnaise, mustard, and lemon juice. Fold in whipped cream and dill. Makes 1-1/2 cups.

Horseradish Cream Sauce

1 tablespoon prepared horseradish
Salt to taste
1 teaspoon sugar

1 teaspoon white vinegar
1 cup heavy cream, whipped

Fold horseradish, salt, sugar, and vinegar into whipped cream.

Basic White Sauce

2 tablespoons butter or margarine   1 cup milk
2 tablespoons flour   Salt and pepper to taste

Melt butter in a saucepan over medium heat. Stir in flour to make a smooth paste. Add milk slowly, stirring constantly until thickened. Cook on low heat for 5 to 10 minutes. Add salt and pepper to taste.

Variations:

Sweetened Sauce: Blend in 1 teaspoon of sugar with flour in basic sauce.
Onion Sauce: Add 1 chopped onion to basic sauce. Cook until tender.
Parsley Sauce: Add 1/2 cup chopped parsley and an extra lump of butter to basic sauce.

Cheese Sauce

1 cup light cream
1 tablespoon butter or margarine
1 cup shredded Danish cheese

(Samsoe, Sevenbo, Havarti)
1 tablespoon cornstarch
1 tablespoon dry white wine

In a saucepan, bring cream and butter to a boil over medium heat. Toss cheese and cornstarch together; add to cream mixture and stir until cheese melts. Blend in wine and stir until smooth. Add paprika.

Variation:

For an entrée, cooked shrimp, chopped ham, or chicken may be added to sauce and served over toast or rice.

Mushroom Sauce

2 cups sliced mushrooms
2 tablespoons butter
2 tablespoons flour
1 cup light cream
Salt to taste

Dash of cayenne pepper
1 cup shredded Tyboe or Samsoe
    cheese (optional)
1 tablespoon dry sherry

Sauté mushrooms in the butter until golden brown. Stir in flour; slowly add the cream. Stirring constantly, reduce heat and simmer until thickened. Add salt and cayenne. If desired, fold in cheese until melted. Add sherry just before serving.

Note: This is good with meats or vegetables, but can also be served over toast as an entrée.

Mustard Sauce

2 tablespoons grainy prepared mustard
1 tablespoon mustard powder
1/4 teaspoon pepper
3/4 teaspoon salt

1/4 cup sugar
Pinch of cardamom
1/4 cup olive oil
1 tablespoon cold water

Blend all ingredients together. Beat until thickened.

Butter-Ginger Sauce

1 teaspoon ground ginger
1/2 cup sugar
1-1/2 teaspoons cornstarch

1/4 cup vinegar
1/4 cup water
3 tablespoons butter

In the top of a double boiler, stir together all ingredients until smooth. Cook until thickened. Especially good on cooked beets.

Sour Cream Gravy

2 tablespoons flour
2 tablespoons butter or drippings
1/2 cup vegetable stock or bouillon

Salt and pepper to taste
1/2 cup sour cream

Stir flour into melted butter or drippings until smooth. Slowly add stock or bouillon, stirring constantly. Reduce heat and cook until thickened. Add seasonings. Stir in sour cream just enough to heat; do not boil.

Note: This is especially good with meatballs.

Tart Brown Gravy

2 tablespoons minced onion	1 bay leaf
2 tablespoons butter or drippings	1 teaspoon prepared mustard
2 tablespoons flour	1/2 teaspoon sugar
1/2 cup stock or bouillon	Salt and pepper to taste

Brown the onion in the melted butter or drippings; add the flour and stir until smooth. Slowly add stock or bouillon, stirring constantly. Add the bay leaf, mustard, sugar, and salt and pepper. Reduce heat and cook until thickened; stir often. Remove bay leaf and/or strain before serving.

Note: A couple spoonfuls of a tart jelly may be added for flavor.

Creamy Danish Blue Cheese Dressing

1/2 cup crumbled Danish blue cheese
1/2 cup mayonnaise
1/2 cup sour cream
1 teaspoon lemon juice

1/4 teaspoon lemon zest
1/2 teaspoon pressed garlic
Pepper to taste
1/3 cup buttermilk (optional)

Blend together all ingredients. Refrigerate at least 3 hours before using.

Note: This is good with cooked or uncooked vegetables.

Sour Cream Dressing

1/2 cup sour cream
1/4 cup mayonnaise
1/2 teaspoon French-style mustard
1/2 teaspoon curry powder

1 tablespoon lemon juice
1/2 teaspoon grated onion
Dash of cayenne pepper

Combine all ingredients. Refrigerate and allow to season for a couple of hours.

Note: This goes well with cooked or uncooked vegetables.

Cakes & Other Desserts

Apple Cake

2 cups sugar
1/2 cup butter
2 eggs
1 teaspoon cinnamon
1/4 teaspoon ground allspice
1/4 teaspoon nutmeg

2 teaspoons baking soda
1/2 teaspoon salt
2 cups sifted flour
1/2 cup walnuts or pecans
4 cups peeled, finely chopped apples

Cream sugar and butter; beat in eggs. Sift together spices, soda, salt, and flour. Add to the creamed mixture. Stir in nuts and apples and mix well. Bake in lightly greased and floured 9x13-inch pan at 350° for 40 to 45 minutes.
Note: This is delicious frosted with a sugar icing or plain, topped with whipped cream or ice cream.

Apple-Crumb Cake (Æblekage)

2 cups well crumbled coconut or soft almond macaroons
1/2 cup butter
1 cup whipping cream
2 tablespoons sugar
2 cups peeled and coarsely chopped eating apples
1/2 cup raspberry jam, thinned with a little water or juice if necessary

Sauté the crumbs in butter over low heat, stirring constantly, long enough for them to absorb the butter. Remove from heat and continue to stir until they cool a little and do not clump together. Whip the cream and sugar until stiff. In a 1-1/2- to 2-quart bowl, arrange alternating layers of buttered crumbs, chopped apple, and whipped cream, making two layers of each. Spoon out like a pudding. Add a dab of jam on each serving for garnish. Serves 6. Best when served immediately, but may be refrigerated.

Danish Layer Cake (Lagkage)

Cake:

4 eggs, separated
3 tablespoons cold water
1 cup sugar
1 (scant) cup all-purpose flour
1-1/2 tablespoons cornstarch
1-1/2 teaspoons baking powder
1/2 teaspoon salt
1 teaspoon vanilla

Filling:

2 cups milk
4 egg yolks, lightly beaten
Pinch of salt
3 tablespoons sugar
1/2 teaspoon vanilla
Raspberry jam or other preserves
Whipped cream for topping

Cake: Beat the four egg yolks until lemon colored. Add water and sugar and beat 2 minutes. Mix and sift the flour, cornstarch, baking powder, and salt. Add

continued

egg yolk mixture and beat well. Beat the egg whites until stiff, then fold into the batter. Stir in vanilla. Bake in four 9-inch ungreased (can be lightly oiled) cake pans (square or round). Bake in a quick, hot oven preheated to 450° for 10 minutes. Cool on racks. **Filling:** Scald milk in top of double boiler; stir in egg yolks and remaining ingredients. Cook until thickened. Cool. Alternate custard or jam between layers. Top with whipped cream.

Note: A variety of fillings may be used.

Sand Cake

1 cup butter
1-1/2 cups sugar
6 eggs, separated

1 cup potato flour, sifted
2 cups all-purpose flour, sifted
1 teaspoon vanilla extract

Cream butter and sugar together. Lightly beat egg yolks; add to creamed mixture a little at a time, beating well after each addition. Add flours and vanilla; mix well. Beat egg whites until stiff, then fold into batter. Pour into lightly oiled and floured 9x13-inch cake pan. Bake 40 to 60 minutes at 350° or until golden brown and cake tests done.

Almond Ring Cake (Kransekage)

Rings:
4 egg whites
4 (8-ounce) cans almond paste
3 cups powdered sugar

White Icing:
1 egg white
1 cup powdered sugar
1/2 teaspoon white vinegar
1/4 cup granulated sugar

In a large bowl, beat egg whites until frothy. Beat in almond paste at low speed a little at a time; continue to beat until mixture is smooth. Slowly add the sugar and beat until mixture is well blended. Draw one 7-1/2 inch circle on heavy bond paper or brown wrapping paper. Using this as a guide, draw eleven more circles, decreasing each circle by 1/2 inch until smallest is about 2 inches in diameter. Grease papers well and place on baking sheets. Use a pastry bag with an opening of about 1 inch and squeeze cake mixture onto pattern circles. Use remaining batter to make two S-shaped curlicues and a star for the top. Bake at 300° for 25 or 30 minutes or until golden. Carefully remove from paper to cool.

To assemble: Pipe icing in a wavy pattern over every other ring. Starting from the bottom, stack rings in graduating circles. Use extra icing to anchor the S-shaped curlicues on two sides at top with star in center.

To serve: Lift off rings and cut or break into desired pieces.

Note: Small clusters of red and green icing on every other ring adds a festive look for the Christmas holidays.

Almond Cake

1/2 cup butter	2-1/2 cups sifted flour
1 cup sugar	2 teaspoons baking powder
4 eggs	3/4 cup milk
1 teaspoon vanilla extract	1/2 cup chopped blanched almonds

Cream butter and sugar together. Add eggs one at a time, beating well after each addition. Stir in vanilla, flour, and baking powder. Blend in the milk and almonds. Pour into lightly oiled ring mold and bake at 350° for 40 to 50 minutes until cake tests done. Turn out to cool. When cool, sprinkle top with powdered sugar.

Fruit Jelly with Cream

1 pound red currants
1/2 pound black currants
1/2 pound cherries or raspberries
3 cups water (approximately)

2-1/2 to 3 tablespoons cornstarch
   per 2 cups liquid
5 to 6 tablespoons sugar
Heavy cream

Layer the cleaned fruit in a saucepan; add just enough water to cover. Slowly bring to a boil and simmer until fruit is thoroughly cooked and juice is a dark red color. Sieve the juice through a clean piece of linen or cheesecloth, pressing as much juice as possible from the berries. Measure the juice and bring to a boil. Dissolve the cornstarch in small amount of water; add 2-1/2 to 3 tablespoons per 2 cups of the boiling juice. Reduce heat, stir, and cook until thickened. Pour into a bowl; sprinkle top with sugar. Chill. Serve cold with heavy cream.

Rum Pudding with Raspberry Sauce

1 package unflavored gelatin
1/4 cup water
4 eggs, separated
2/3 cup sugar
1-1/2 ounces rum

1/2 pint whipping cream, whipped
Raspberry Sauce:
1 pint frozen, sweetened raspberries
1 tablespoon cornstarch
1 tablespoon water

Soak gelatin in the water; dissolve over hot water. Beat egg yolks and sugar until lemon colored. Combine gelatin and egg mixture; add the rum and let stand. Beat egg whites until stiff; fold into thickened gelatin mixture, then fold in the whipped cream. Chill until firm. **Sauce:** Bring raspberries to a boil. Reduce heat and simmer, covered, for about 5 minutes. Strain and discard pulp. Blend cornstarch and water; stir into juice. Stir and cook until mixture thickens. Chill before serving.

Rhubarb Custard

1-1/2 pounds fresh rhubarb
1 cup sugar
1/2 cup water
1 tablespoon cornstarch
Custard:
1 package unflavored gelatin

1/4 cup cold water
2 eggs
2 tablespoons sugar
1 cup milk
1 tablespoon vanilla extract
Whipped cream for topping

Chop rhubarb (about 2-inch pieces). Bring sugar and water to a boil; add rhubarb and simmer until almost tender. Remove saucepan from heat and place rhubarb in a serving bowl. Mix cornstarch with a small amount of cold water and stir into liquid. Return to heat and simmer for about 3 minutes until thickened. Pour over rhubarb and mix carefully. **Prepare custard:** Soften gelatin in the cold water. In a

continued

Rhubarb Custard *continued*

saucepan, beat eggs and sugar together until fluffy. Heat milk to boiling point and add to egg mixture; beat thoroughly. Stirring constantly, simmer until thickened. Stir in vanilla and softened gelatin. Pour custard over the rhubarb. Chill and serve with whipped cream.

Note: Place some of the red rhubarb pieces on top for a festive look.

Rice Pudding with Raisins

1/2 cup long-grained white rice
1 cup lightly salted boiling water
4 cups whole milk
1/4 cup butter
3 eggs
1/4 cup sugar

1 cup plump raisins
1/2 teaspoon vanilla
Topping:
3 tablespoons sugar
1 tablespoon cinnamon

Pour rice slowly into boiling water; cover tightly and cook 7 minutes. Add the milk and butter and bring to a boil. Cover and cook on low heat for about 1 hour. Beat eggs and sugar together; add raisins and vanilla. Gently stir egg mixture into rice mixture, stirring until thickened. Mix sugar and cinnamon together and sprinkle over top of each serving.

Rice Pudding with Almonds

3-1/2 cups milk
3-1/2 tablespoons sugar
3/4 cup white long-grained rice
1 cup chopped blanched almonds

1/3 cup sherry wine
2 teaspoons vanilla
1/2 pint heavy cream, whipped
1 whole almond (optional)

(Ris al' amande)

Bring milk to a boil. Slowly add the sugar and rice; stir and lower heat. Simmer uncovered for 30 minutes until rice is tender. Pour cooked rice into a bowl, then add the chopped almonds, sherry, and vanilla. Allow to cool. Fold whipped cream into the rice mixture. (If the occasion calls for the tradition of finding the "lucky" almond, mix in one whole almond. The one served the pudding containing the almond wins a prize or a wish for good luck.)

Lemon Snow (Citron Fromage)

1 package unflavored gelatin
1/2 cup cold water
3 eggs, separated
1 cup sugar

Juice and grated rind of 1 lemon
1 cup orange juice
1 cup whipping cream, whipped

Dissolve gelatin in the cold water. Slightly beat egg yolks; add sugar and beat until thick and lemon colored. Add juices and the grated lemon rind. Cook in top of a double boiler until thickened. Mix the dissolved gelatin into the cooked mixture. Cool. Beat egg whites until stiff but not dry and fold into the cooled mixture. Refrigerate until thoroughly cooled but not set. Whip cream until it forms peaks, then fold into pudding mixture. Return to refrigerator until firm. Serve with dabs of whipped cream if desired.

Caramel Pudding

Caramel Sauce:
1 cup sugar
1 cup boiling water
2 cups whipped cream

Pudding:
2 cups heavy cream
5 eggs
1/4 cup sugar
1 teaspoon vanilla

Caramel sauce: Melt sugar in a skillet until brown; do not burn. Pour half of this into a warmed mold, coating the inside of mold. Pour 1 cup of boiling water over sugar remaining in skillet and simmer until most of liquid is dissolved. Cool. Add whipped cream just before serving. **Pudding:** Heat cream to boiling point but do not boil. Beat eggs, sugar, and vanilla together until frothy. Add to the hot cream. Pour mixture through a fine strainer, then pour into the caramel-coated mold. Set mold over a kettle of boiling water and let simmer until firm, about 20 to 30 minutes. Cool thoroughly. Mix whipped cream with the caramel sauce and serve with the pudding.

Poor Knights

8 slices white bread
1 cup milk
4 tablespoons sugar
1 teaspoon cinnamon

Butter
Fruit sauce of choice
1 tablespoon cornstarch

Soak bread in the milk. Combine sugar and cinnamon and sprinkle over each slice of bread. Melt butter in a skillet and fry bread until golden brown.

To make a fruit sauce: Thaw package of frozen fruit of choice and drain juice into a saucepan. Mix cornstarch with a little cold water; stir into juice and cook until thickened. Stir fruit into mixture, just to heat. Serve warm over the "Poor Knights."

Buttermilk Dessert

1 tablespoon unflavored gelatin
1/4 cup cold water
1 cup sugar
1 teaspoon vanilla extract

2 cups buttermilk
Juice of 1 orange
1 tablespoon orange zest
1 cup whipping cream, whipped

Dissolve gelatin in water in the top of a double boiler. Stir in sugar and heat until dissolved. Add vanilla. Mix buttermilk, orange juice, and orange zest. Stir into the gelatin mixture and chill just until mixture begins to set. Fold in whipped cream and chill until firm.

Gooseberry Pie

Crust:
1/2 cup lard or vegetable shortening
1-1/2 cups all-purpose flour
1/2 teaspoon salt
1/2 tablespoon vinegar
2-1/2 tablespoons cold water
1 small egg

Filling:
4 cups fresh gooseberries
1-1/2 cups sugar
4 tablespoons flour
1 tablespoon tapioca
Juice of 1 lemon
Butter

Crust: Cut shortening into the flour; add salt, vinegar, and water. Beat egg slightly and mix into dough. Roll out two crusts on a lightly floured surface. Press bottom crust into pie baking dish. **Filling:** Mix all filling ingredients, except butter, together and let stand for about 20 minutes, then pour into unbaked pie shell. Dot with butter and cover with top crust. Crimp edges and cut slits to allow steam to escape. Bake in preheated 450° oven for 15 minutes; reduce heat to 350° and bake 45 minutes more.

Cookies

Coconut Macaroons (Kokosmakroner)

3 eggs
1 cup sugar
1 tablespoon butter, softened

3 cups finely shredded coconut
1/2 cup flour

Thoroughly mix eggs, sugar, and softened butter together. Stir in coconut and flour. Drop teaspoonsful on well-greased cookie sheet. Bake in 350° oven until lightly browned and holds shape when removed from sheet, about 8 to 10 minutes.

Medal Cakes (Medaljekager)

Cakes:
2-1/4 cups all-purpose flour
1/2 cup powdered sugar
2 egg yolks
1 cup butter
Custard:
2 cups milk

2 egg yolks, lightly beaten
2-1/2 tablespoons sugar
Pinch of salt
1/2 teaspoon vanilla extract
2 tablespoons cornstarch
4 marshmallows

Combine flour and powdered sugar. Lightly beat egg yolks; add to dry mixture. Knead in the butter. Let rest in a cold place for 30 minutes. On a lightly floured surface, roll out thin and cut into rounds. Place on lightly greased baking sheets and bake until golden brown in a 350° oven, about 8 minutes. Cool on a rack.

Prepare custard: Heat the milk. Add egg yolks, sugar, salt, vanilla, and cornstarch (mixed with a little cold water). Stir in the marshmallows until melted.

Assembly: Put two cakes together with custard between. If desired, cover tops with powdered sugar icing to which a lemon or almond flavoring has been added.

Spritz Cookie (Sprutter)

1 cup butter
2/3 cup sugar
3 egg yolks

1 teaspoon almond extract
2 cups all-purpose flour

Cream together the butter and sugar. Mix in remaining ingredients until dough is smooth. Place dough in a cookie press and shape as desired on a well-greased cookie sheet. Bake in a hot, 375° to 400° oven for 10 to 12 minutes until lightly browned. Watch carefully for they brown easily. Cool on racks.

Danish Anise Seed Cookies

1/2 cup butter
1 cup sugar
4 egg yolks
1 teaspoon vanilla

1-1/2 cups flour
2 teaspoons baking powder
1/3 teaspoon salt
1 tablespoon anise seeds

Cream together the butter and sugar. Beat in egg yolks (reserve a little for brushing tops); add vanilla. Sift in the flour, baking powder, salt, and anise seeds. Roll out on a lightly floured surface to 1/4 inch thickness. Cut into desired shapes and brush tops with beaten egg yolk. Place on greased baking sheets and bake at 350° for 15 minutes.

Molasses Cookies

1/2 cup melted shortening
1/2 cup molasses
2 tablespoons milk
1 tablespoon grated lemon rind
2 cups all-purpose flour

1/2 teaspoon baking soda
1/2 teaspoon salt
1/2 teaspoon ground ginger
1/2 teaspoon cinnamon

Mix shortening, molasses, milk, and lemon rind together. Sift in remaining ingredients and mix well. Chill dough slightly before rolling out to 1/8 inch thickness on a lightly floured surface. Cut into rounds and place on a lightly greased baking sheet. Bake at 400° for about 8 minutes. Cool on racks. Do not stack until thoroughly cooled.

Sand Tarts

1/2 cup butter
1 cup sugar
2 eggs, separated
1-1/2 cups all-purpose flour
1 teaspoon baking powder

1/2 teaspoon salt
Topping:
Split almonds
1 tablespoon sugar
1/4 teaspoon cinnamon

Cream butter, sugar, two egg yolks, and one egg white together. Sift in flour, baking powder, and salt. Mix until well blended to make a firm dough; add a little more flour if necessary. Chill on lightly floured surface and roll to 1/4 inch thickness. Cut into star shapes. Place split almond on each cookie and brush with remaining unbeaten egg white. Combine sugar and cinnamon; sprinkle on cookies. Place on lightly greased baking sheets and bake at 375° for 10 minutes. Cool.

Butter Balls

1 cup butter
3 tablespoons powdered sugar
1 teaspoon vanilla

2 cups flour
1 cup finely chopped nuts
Powdered sugar for dusting

Cream together the butter, powdered sugar, and vanilla. Mix in the flour and nuts. Shape into small balls and bake on an ungreased baking sheet at 350° for 20 minutes. Roll in powdered sugar while still warm.

Peppernuts (Pebbernødder)

1 cup butter or margarine
2 cups sugar
3 teaspoons vanilla
4 eggs

1/3 cup heavy cream
4 teaspoons baking powder
6 cups all-purpose flour
2 teaspoons salt

Cream together butter and sugar. Add vanilla. Beat in eggs one at a time. Add cream alternately with mixture of the baking powder, flour, and salt. Divide dough into four parts and roll out each part to 1/4 inch thickness on a lightly floured surface. Stack parts with waxed paper between and chill overnight. Cut into 1/4-inch cubes. Bake on ungreased baking sheet at 350° for about 12 minutes until light brown. **Hint:** Cutting directly on the baking sheet facilitates spacing the cubes about 1 inch apart.

Meringue Kisses (Marengs)

4 egg whites
1-1/3 cups powdered sugar

2 teaspoons vinegar
1/4 teaspoon salt

Beat egg whites until stiff. Continue to beat while adding sugar gradually. When quite stiff, beat in vinegar and salt. Continue beating until very stiff and dry. Using a pastry tube or teaspoon, shape into mounds about the size of a quarter. Drop onto waxed paper that has been placed on a cookie sheet. Bake in a very slow, 200° to 250° oven for at least 50 minutes. Let cool a little, but remove from paper while still warm.

Old-Fashioned Sugar Cookies

4-1/2 cups sifted flour
1 teaspoon salt
1 teaspoon baking soda
1 teaspoon baking powder
1 cup butter

1-1/2 cups sugar
2 eggs
1 cup sour cream
1-1/2 teaspoons vanilla
Sugar for sprinkling tops

Mix flour, salt, baking soda, and baking powder. Cream butter and sugar; beat in eggs one at a time. Add dry ingredients alternately with the sour cream and mix until smooth. Blend in the vanilla. Chill dough until firm. Roll out on a lightly floured surface and cut into desired shapes with a cookie cutter. Sprinkle with sugar and bake on lightly greased baking sheets at 350° for about 12 minutes, until done. Cool on racks.

Danish Pan Cookies

1 cup sugar
1 cup butter
1 teaspoon vanilla
2 cups all-purpose flour

1/2 teaspoon salt
1 egg, separated
1/2 cup chopped nuts

Cream the sugar and butter. Add vanilla. Sift the flour and salt together into butter mixture. Dough should be stiff. Pat out on an ungreased 10x15-inch baking sheet. Beat one egg white until foamy. Brush on top of dough and sprinkle with the chopped nuts. Bake 45 minutes in a 300° oven. Cut into squares while hot. Makes 3 dozen.

Fried Twists (Klejner)

3 eggs

1 cup sugar

1/2 teaspoon salt

1/4 cup heavy cream

1 teaspoon baking powder

1/2 cup melted butter

1 teaspoon vanilla

1/2 teaspoon cardamom

2-1/2 to 3 cups flour, divided

Vegetable oil or fat for deep-frying

Beat eggs and sugar until light; add salt, cream, and baking powder. Stir in melted butter, vanilla, cardamom, and about 3/4 cup of the flour. Stir in enough of the remaining flour to make a batter stiff enough to roll out when chilled. Chill, then roll out on a lightly floured surface to 3/16 inch thickness. (Too much flour makes *klejner* tough.) Cut into diamond shapes about 2-1/2 inches long. Cut a slit in center and pull one end through slit. Fry in deep fat heated to 400° until golden brown. Drain on paper towels. Makes about 10 dozen.

Drinks

Boiled Coffee with Egg

1 egg, slightly beaten
1 eggshell, crushed
1/2 cup cold water

1/2 cup regular grind coffee
Pinch of salt
6 cups boiling water

Mix in a coffeepot (or saucepan with a tight-fitting lid) the egg, eggshell, 1/2 cup cold water, coffee, and salt. Stir thoroughly, then add 6 cups boiling water. Over moderate heat, bring to the boiling point and simmer for about 3 minutes. Reduce heat to low and allow to steep without boiling.

Note: If using a pot with a spout, plug the spout to hold in the full aroma of the coffee. Adding 1/2 cup cold water before steeping aids clearing.

Christmas Punch (Fancy Gløgg)

2 quarts claret wine
2 quarts port wine
3 tablespoons candied orange peel
20 cardamom seeds
25 whole cloves

6 cinnamon sticks
1 pound blanched almonds
1 pound seedless raisins
1 pound sugar lumps
2 cups cognac

Heat wines in a large enamel container. Place the orange peel, cardamom seeds, cloves, and cinnamon sticks in a cheesecloth bag and boil slowly in the wine. After about 20 minutes, add the almonds and raisins to the brew and boil slowly for 20 minutes more. Remove from heat and discard the spice bag. Place sugar lumps in a fine wire strainer. Slowly pour the cognac over the sugar. Light a match and hold it near the sugar to ignite the cognac. When all the sugar has melted, remove the strainer and cover the container with a lid to put out the flame. Serve hot with a few almonds and raisins in each mug. Serves about 40.

Note: For a dramatic presentation, you may wish to add the flaming sugar just before serving.

New Year's Eve Punch

1-3/4 cups sugar
3-1/2 cups water
2 cinnamon sticks

1 teaspoon whole cloves
1 quart apple cider
6 cups strong brewed tea

Boil the sugar and water together to make a syrup. Place cinnamon and cloves in a cheesecloth bag. Combine the syrup, spice bag, cider, and tea and let stand overnight. Serve cold or heated. Serves about 20.

Cherry Liqueur

2 pounds sweet red cherries, with
    pits (dark Bing or other)
1-3/4 cups sugar

2-3/4 cups vodka
1-1/4 cups brandy

Wash and stem cherries, then cut each cherry to open slightly and place them into glass containers with tight-fitting lids. Mix the sugar, vodka, and brandy together until sugar is dissolved. Pour the liquid mixture over the cherries; stir and cover tightly. Let age in a cool, dark place. For the first 2 weeks, stir frequently, then let age a minimum of 3 months for best flavor. Strain off liqueur; discard cherries. Strain again if needed for clarity. Bottle as desired.

List of Recipes

Danish Immigrant Museum
Elk Horn, Iowa

Photographs

Front cover: Æbleskiver pan with æbleskiver
Royal Copenhagen Blue-Fluted dinnerware

Inside front cover: Trivoli Fest parade past the
Danish Windmill, Elk Horn, Iowa

Inside back cover: Photograph shows a Kimballton,
Iowa, replica of the Little Mermaid from the
Copenhagen harbor. Another replica is in Solvang,
California. Busts of Hans Christian Andersen, who
wrote *The Little Mermaid*, are in Elk Horn, Iowa, and
Solvang.

Back cover: Danish folk dancers from Kimballton, Iowa,
on stage at the Tivoli Fest, Elk Horn

BOOKS BY MAIL Stocking Stuffers Postpaid You may mix titles. One book for $12.95; two for $21.00; three for $29.00; four for $36.00; six for $52.00; twelve for $95.00. 2009 Prices subject to change.

Æbleskiver and More (Danish)
American Gothic Cookbook
Amish Mennonite Recipes
  && Traditions
Buffets and Potlucks
Cherished Czech Recipes
Czech & Slovak Kolaches
  && Sweet Treats
Dandy Dutch Recipes
Dear Danish Recipes
Dutch Style Recipes
Fine Finnish Foods
French Recipes
German Style Recipes
Great German Recipes

Healthy Recipes
Microwave Recipes
Norwegian Centennial Recipes
Norwegian Recipes
Pleasing Polish Recipes
Quality Czech Mushroom Recipes
Quality Dumpling Recipes
Recipes from Ireland
Recipes from Old Mexico
Savory Scottish Recipes
Scandinavian Holiday Recipes
Scandinavian Smorgasbord Recipes
Scandinavian Sweet Treats
Scandinavian Style Fish and Seafood
Slavic Specialties

Slovak Recipes
Splendid Swedish Recipes
Tales from Texas Tables
Texas Cookoff
Time-Honored Norwegian Recipes
Ukrainian Recipes
Waffles, Flapjacks, Pancakes from
  Scandinavia and Around the World

License to Cook Series:

Alaska Style; Arizona Style;
Iowa Style; Italian Style;
Minnesota Style; Missouri Style;
New Mexico Style;
Oregon Style; Texas Style;
and Wisconsin Style

PENFIELD BOOKS, 215 BROWN STREET, IOWA CITY, IA 52245-5801 • 1-800-728-9998 • www.penfieldbooks.com